A Barrel of Monkeys

Poems selected from
The 1000 Monkeys Competition 2016
with additional contributions from guest poets.

Edited by Janice Windle

First Edition

1st June 2016

ISBN: 978-1-907435-28-7

Published by Dempsey & Windle

Front cover photograph by Dónall Dempsey

Illustrations by Janice Windle

Photo of Susan Evans by Andrew King

Photo of Andy V Frost by Ant Smith

© Copyright remains with all the individual contributors to this collection, who have asserted their ownership and given their permission to Dempsey & Windle for their poems to be published here.

All rights reserved. No part of this publication may be reproduced, stored in a retrieval system or transmitted in any form or by any means without the written consent of Dempsey&Windle (dempseyandwindle.co.uk), nor otherwise circulated in any form of binding or cover other than that in which it is published and without a similar condition being imposed on a subsequent purchaser.

dempseyandwindle.co.uk

CONTENTS

2016 COMPETITION WINNERS

We're indebted to Alwyn Marriage for selecting the winners of The 1000 Monkeys' competition:

First place:

The First Day of November by Richard Sellwood

Second place:
Simplifying my Mother by Ray Diamond

Joint third place:
North by Geoffrey Pimlott
Youth by John Wheeler

Commended:
What the Butler Saw by Ray Diamond
At the Chemist by Caro Reeves

Editor's commendations:
This Summer by Karen Izod
The Elephant in the Room by Trisha Broomfield

All the winning and long-listed poems are in the first section of this anthology.

A Barrel of Monkeys

Monkey Minds

habilis, erectus. Sapiens
finally, one of them

saw time for what it was.
But for the rest of us

(with minds formed to gauge
the edibility of leaves

and the use of lianes
to swing from tree to tree)

time still comes in lines, life
in boxes of dates.

Sarah Watkinson

The Ayenbite of Inwyt

The Ayenbite of Inwyt might be Sultan
Of some hot, moist eastern island,
Who drowses on a golden throne
And is fanned with peacock feathers.

Or it might be a wild, tormented sea,
That runs between two craggy spits of land,
Dashing ships against the jagged rocks
And drawing men down into its cold embrace.

But the Ayenbite is neither of these things.
The Ayenbite is a hairy little monster
That bites your toes beneath the bedclothes,
Makes them twitch and then curl backwards.

It knows what you have left undone,
And what you have done that you shouldn't.
It pushes its pointed snout into your ear
And whispers them, one by one.

It rifles through drifts of memory with its claws,
Raking up deeds you wanted to forget.
You toss and turn among the tangled sheets.
You cannot sleep: it will not let you sleep.

A Barrel of Monkeys

**If you are perfect in all you do and say,
You need not fear the Ayenbite of Inwyt, but,
If you are not, put the pillow over your head,
Count to a thousand, and remember that**

The morning brings not just light, but indifference.

Lorri Pimlott

The Ayenbite of Inwyt (The inner sting of conscience) is actually a 14th century confessional book, translated from the original French into a Kentish dialect.

The Dark Is Neither Wrong Nor Right

"Proclaimed the time was neither wrong or right

I have been one acquainted with the night."

Robert Frost.

The jury is still out, my friend,
Daniel cannot come to judgment,
he snores,
let Daniel sleep,
meanwhile, come let us converse
with the dark of the night.

The dark, my friend
is neither wrong or right,
it lets the star sing on.

At dusk, it was I
who hung the sun out to dry.
It singed till
it burned itself out.

For now, let us not judge,
let us not search
for a plausible reason why,
the moon maybe ambivalent,
maybe it is not the catalyst or
an accomplice of our nocturnal mishaps,

maybe this fickle mindedness
stems from within us?

Daniel snores,
Twilight tiptoes
to dawn.
Case adjourned.

Colonel Shyam Sunder Sharma,Shaurya Chakra (Rtd)

Outside

Outside.
Beneath the sky,
Above the earth,
I stand.

The sea-soft dark wave-sprayed with fingertipping stars.

Seek out the points of light
Bright Sirius...Orion's belt... the way across the heaven to the pole
and I
the smallest ripple on an ocean sky
stand here,
and look.

I know the chalky dawn will rub away the night.
Cloud-shroud its dust-blown bubble round another day.
And I will live again with
old news traffic lights rice congealing in the sink those voices from so long ago:

"Yes! You should know your place lad!"

As though they knew their own and I did not.
Perhaps it's true.
I didn't know my place out in the sun.

But here,
right now,
beneath the sky,
above the earth,
I do.

John Wheeler

This summer

I remember a June morning much like this -
1 was 27, maybe 28, setting off, letter in hand.
I wore my new pink dress, its dots and dashes
tight at the waist.

Swirling I went, up to town.
I rarely went to London – let
alone – those silent corridors, Freud
solemn on his pedestal.

They had us writing about shapes,
shadows, telling a story,
though it was not an interview for a poet.
So much easier to talk about people

in-spite of the video, the one-way screen.
This is 20 years ago, I realise.
I loved that dress, the excitement,
the *'I have it all to come'* feeling,

as I sat, face backwards on the train,
in the hope I was looking at a future.

So this morning, as the sun glints
On the wet grass, and my mind fills
with the sounds of summer
then I want all that back.
Some sense of what is to come,
some seeking of the thrill.

Karen Izod

What The Butler Saw

I have an electronic picture frame
Hanging in my dining room,
Thousands of photos of myself
In chronological order
From infant to incipient old age
Each one dissolving into the next
New born, mouth covered in jam
Taking my first steps; wielding a cricket bat
Strutting the boards in a school play
Longhaired and rebellious at university
Passport shot in later life looking a shade more bitter
Transitions almost seamless, but with a hint of flicker
Like an end of pier What the Butler Saw
Or an early silent film
And in a dead language on the rim
To be used as a reminder and a warning
Not *Carpe Diem*
But *Timor Mortis Conturbat Me*
The fear of death oppresses me

Ray Diamond

Memories

Memories drop in like old friends
With shared thoughts
To visit the crowded city,
The city of no gates.
They wander in through a veil
Tearing down old barriers
Where the security of time past
Means little.
It's open house –
You may look but don't touch
Your presence may worry me too much.

Ray Pool

The Big Bang

Does that skeleton feel and see?
Is it disturbed?
Alongside trinkets, broken pots, carbon dated teeth,
This permanent smile reveals a violent death,
Here the axe wounds that severed his existence.

Did he ever contemplate?
Was he occupied with banality?
Like "I wonder what we're having to eat later?
Does she love me? Are you really my friend?"
Did he ever struggle with a runny egg yolk?

The meat has gone now,
Just the dry bones left, separated,
Moved by maggot movements
And those attracted to
The stench that freezes over.

Then the melting releases the anxiety,
The fossil past, images held In solid rock,
A time when my memories walked the earth,
An extinct species, tended tenderly in
Glass cases 'do not touch the exhibits'

As permafrost thaws
It releases a dangerous gas, a destructive force,
And my face and limbs imprinted in the stone,
Long forgotten the taste of the fruit
That grew from my leftovers.

And the sun creeps gently closer, closer, closer,
That final act that will incinerate the evidence,
Reduced down to a single bright star
For the entertainment of another
Wide eye through another telescope.

James Carter

Into the Black

Dark, darkling, silent scream,
Fast watching, awaiting the night,
The black, bleak insistent calling
Of an answerless question
That creeps without light.
Pitched in the squall
Of a dim distant storm
The candle spent
The song drowned out
And all that is left
Is an echo-less shout.

Joy Parry Collins

Year 3 are doing Music and Movement

Being aeroplanes, windmills, falling leaves
until the moment Major segues into Minor
and they stop,
lost in the slow chords vibrating through them
which summon ghosts
who dance among them
show them how to drift and flit
demonstrate the choreography of haunting,
reaching, searching, waving their goodbyes
to something far-off,
fast-receding, lost.

Rochelle Parker

Simplifying My Mother

I'm attempting to simplify my mother

Going through her cupboards
Unwrapping bag within bag
In her dust-laden bedroom

Finding the odd photo
A faded guarantee
A broken hanger
A scrap of paper
With an address or name

A glove or lotion preserved
For some special occasion
Which never came

I could draw my mother's decline
On a map of her local area -
Circles or contour lines
Of smaller and smaller radius

Blackberry bushes recede
Becoming unreachable

Benches where we would rest
Too tiring to attain

Finally, the centre
And circumference the same

Ray Diamond

By the Radiator

I stole some midget gems.
I felt sick when I ate them.
Because they were yours,
And you had cancer.

You said I've got six weeks to live.
I said Dad you won't see us grow up.
I said it for effect,
I said it to make you cry.

You watched Countdown
And did crosswords
After you returned from chemo,
Your face cut with tears,

Back hunched by the radiator.
I wanted to watch Neighbours.
I sat in my room smoking
Wondering how to tell you

I loved you.
They took you away at night.
I think I was sleeping.
I don't like midget gems.

Alicia Buller

Exemplar

He lays his head on my lap.
Even if he's asleep, the tip of his tail
responds when I say, *sweet dog.*

I respect his sense of Dog. I tell you
he pleases me more than the one
with a certificate for obedience.

He's always known his duty.
He watches the gate for a chance to slip off
find a mate and make more dogs.

We have called in darkening woods
run across empty fields, telephoned
neighbours, police and the dog pound -

it is deplorable. But I admire
his solid self-belief, like honour,
his epaulettes of gold fur and his legends.

Sarah Watkinson

You got the jitters

You are scared of trains
buses
planes
ISIS
kids that kick bottles
the pimple on your foot
next week's deadlines
war
bankruptcy
mugging
the woman you sit next to
cats and dogs
the London Underground
failure
six-inch beards.

On Sundays something
Gnaws at your stomach.
And when you sleep
The pain gets worse.

So you eat more,
Laugh,
Make plans,

A Barrel of Monkeys

Sleep with people.

You buy a country cottage
Porsche Cayman
Cayman Islands
Apple Macs
Leather sofas
Conservatory
Swimming pool.

You ride horses,
Take up jogging,
Join aqua-aerobics.
You host dinner parties
Sink into sweet obliteration.

On Sunday evenings
Your gut wrenches;
It's being spooned out
Like a bottomless yoghurt.

You are scared of wrinkles,
Grey in your roots,
Yellow in your skin,
Veins on your legs,
Lard chunks on your booty.

A Barrel of Monkeys

You buy Bose everything,
something from Prada,
an advance iPhone 6s,
your favourite perfume,
a therapist for this
and guru for that.

You join a yoga class,
Buy parquet flooring,
An automated garage,
Nintendo Wii for the kids.

You're sick more often these days.
So you buy brand-new everything
And eat organic food.
You're scared of
AIDS
BSC
SARS
Anthrax
Old people
The wrong shampoo.
You take up the trampoline,
Learn origami,
Paint watercolours,
Get a life-counsellor.

A Barrel of Monkeys

On Sunday evening
You're sick in the bed.
You dreamt of a black
Pit where you walked
Without aim.

You heard a bat's flutter,
And a drip-drip-drip
that wouldn't stop.
The ground rocked.
There was no way out.

Your knees shook
And you began to cry,
Because there was nothing.
There was no one.

Alicia Buller

The Bee Lesson

A young boy on a stump
cupped in his hand
the carcass of a bumble bee.

Walking home he found a
bumble bee unable to
fly with an injured wing,

He took it home
set up a jar with grass and
sticks, dirt and honey

So the bee could mend
and fly again

So the boy could do
good in the world.

Left outside, overnight
on a stump
the boy returned and

A Barrel of Monkeys

Ants had found the
honey and the bee,
had eaten the bee, inside-out

A hollow shell without
its little bee heart,
the boy, horrified, sad.

The bee lesson then:
good intentions mean nothing
plans go wrong
death is a part of life.

The bee lesson now;
it's ok if an injured bee
is used to feed hungry ants.

Kyle McHale

Cupid

The heart
a bloody fist.
Breaking cages made of bone
by bludgeoning the body with blows
that fall like heavy stone.
Blood buried by birth
is born of pierced skin.
The slain now lie in love.
The cherub is not a child,
he is a man fit for war.

Ivor Hartney

Linley Beeches – A Shropshire Hill

(after Housman)

A wood in trouble on Wenlock Edge,
The Wrekin heaves its forest fleece,
But further west a storm is brewing,
Which cracks and breaks a Linley beech.

Two centuries past the avenue triumphed,
Beech trees planted on Linley Hill
Growing strong against the west wind
Standing proud for years until ...

Arthritic now the branches creak
With every passing summer breeze
And when the wind blows strong in winter
Dry wood is torn from rigid trees.

Limbs lie broken on the hillside,
Roots like fingers reach for the sky
Trunks lie prone like fallen soldiers,
But these proud trees refuse to die.

Aged trees, unbending, broken,
Unable to move with changing times,
Like ancient earthworks built by Offa,
Relics of strength on a Shropshire hillside.

Kathy Tytler

Green

(after Edward Thomas)

There is no green like the green of spring
No billiard baize, no emerald ring
No rolling sea, nor any thing
Is green like the green of an English spring.

There is no green like the green of spring
No knife so sharp, no blade so keen
No eye of cat has quite that zing.
No, nothing but the green of spring
Can stir the choirs within to sing
And lift us high upon the wings
Of beauty.

There is no green like the green of spring.

Jeremy Loynes

Rookery

A winter field is flooded, iced
bare frost chills the air;
at the border beneath withered Elms
words are muttered in the dusk

as the February birds settle
into a dark resting at night,
their trees cloud shadowed
with a language of coldness

by a guttural croak
as if stuck in the throat.
This city of silhouetted branches
protectorate of eggs against sterile weathers,

an east wind as orange day breaks,
birds swarm black in the matins sky
charting ancestral paths over wood, field or town
speaking as if the air is a love charm.

Richard Sellwood

The Last Day of November

On this last day of November
I have looked back at snow

on the bitter east wind. Out of
windows watched lashing rain

carry its dirge across the dark
valley, grey clouds shifting

their mist up the mountains.
This last day, the river's flood

surging, whirling down rocks
to fall, this end of month time,

moor grass blowing cold
before winter's plunge,

into a mirror of red, dead leaves
as late daylight sun plays

on a stand of birch trees,
leaving ghostwhite shimmering

in the sour brooding sky of
this last November day.

Richard Sellwood

North

the north emerged from the clouds
and swirled about future's
rain falling all day
homemade hats and banners
set the morning pretty
complaining down the grey damp street
because a lot turned out
before the rain became
yet despite a bad dawn
the north marched moors and dales
of discontent in swoops and swerves
dips and climbs the forecast warm
and dry but not until protest
soaked in bad weather's discontent
then clouds clear mumbling the bleak sky
crawl back forgotten in the great divide
not to question or wonder why
the north swirled rain-torn's dark day
or give a clout that that lot turned out
complaining hats and banners

Geoffrey Pimlott

The Northern Line

That black line running deep beneath London
runs deep
in me.

Deeper than the line I could draw with my finger
on the dirty wooden sills of '38 stock
before Grandmother's
or Mother's slap
would stop me in my tracks.

Deeper than the Wandle,
flowing below and beside New Merton Board Mills.
My father worked there
under the shadow of that ugly grey tower block
at Colliers Wood.

Deeper than the foundations
for the flyovers and roadworks of the North Circular
at Staples Corner and the start of the M1
where my Grandfather travelled to for so long via
Edgware
to repair the trench diggers and pile drivers that made
them.
Deeper than Screen 3 at the Piccadilly Plaza
with a late night showing

of a good new film
to ice and cherry a great day out
around Soho and Leicester Square.

Deeper than the poetry
that I would travel in to hear
in Central or Northern, East End or West End
before drinking long and deep into the night
with like-minded friends.

That black line running deep beneath London
runs deep
in me.

Andy V Frost

Lord Nelson (born 1926)

Lord Nelson and me
on a summer's ride
in the crook of his arm
through the countryside

I stood while he huffed
and stood while he puffed
in his green shiny coat
he shovelled the miles
and hot he ran with his iron will

and we rode like the Lord
and we're riding still.

Ray Pool

Youth

They came aboard the train, a bubbling group
each with a sharpened ringtone voice too loud
They occupied the seats, a gaggling troup,
a half-formed riot, a dayglo-blooded crowd.
The laughing insults flew obscenely round.
The diamond lipstick, sharp as any joke,
The flops of hair, the tee-shirts, and the ground
they shared as easily as sharing coke.
I hated them, then slowly wondered why.
Perhaps, I'd never known this easy run
of camaraderie; my youth, too shy.
In truth, I knew I loved them, every one.
I saw my face caught in the window glare
and told my aging eyes, I didn't care.

John Wheeler

In The Coffee Bar

Tight bright sweater, dark spiky hair,
lap-top open, smart-phone turned on.
His loud voice dominates, the lesson begins.
Sitting opposite, the younger silent colleague,
note pad open, pen poised eagerly,
desperate to learn written all over her face.
Mr Been There and Back wants to impress,
Miss Long Way To Go wants to arrive.

I, the observer, see who I once was.

Owen Osler

DanceVoice

We are Birds of Passion,
In the Quaker meeting house in Wedmore Vale.
We shed our outdoor coats to reveal the loose old clothes
we've worn all day
in preparation
soon we will spin
decked with glittery threads and feather boas
stretch into our shadows, in concentrated focus behind
paper-mache masks.
In the beginning we were stiff,
frowns stapled to our foreheads,
the days' weight made us
elephantine

The tutor gave us
the room in a two step waltz, her calm, strong voice
restored lost flexibility – we moved
despite ourselves.
We are
Laban and Martha Graham, we are free form and bound
freeze in motion, hear the traffic's lumbering drone
outside
Freed from the clay
of expectation, we are blood and bone, heart and ankle
and at our core, the centre of all gravity
this serious joy.

Pauline Sewards

Barcelona

Like a child, I plead 'are we nearly there?'
on the Barcelona boulevard that Poet Lorca
wished would never end. La Rambla then,
all tree-lined promenade; no tourist tat.
We're in search of La Boqueria, where our dear
Food-writer friend, Kat said we simply must go
devour the best seafood in all the world...
we twirl past theatres and bars; tickled by the
temptation of `show-time' yet famished, too
aware of seafood fare on the horizon – pause now
we might give in to a dirty burger. Third of way
down, side street leads to seduction of the senses,
a kind of Covent Garden food hall; stalls cascading
fruits, and there our seafood promise – a grand
design of the cockle shed. Bar-stools surround
shutters down – we're too late, yet strangely happy
to have found this. Head across to tapas bar, wine
produced an hour away. Partake of the grape with
authentic lid-sized bread, cheese, olives – we stay
a while; feeling like true artisans. Before swaying
back to boutique hotel, loving Lorca's La Rambla –
sated, inebriated; happier now. We bimble into
Beethoven's store; listen to every score on tiny, tin,
tune drum; endless fun. Our giddy hearts carry
home Debussy's *Clair de Lune*.

Susan Evans

The Homecoming

I sailed in on the Nonpareil, my arms outstretched like wings
and threw my bag onto a horse drawn cart – no label required
I stepping stoned my way across the bay on boulders slick and wet
stopping to pop bladder vraic between finger and thumb,
delighting in its viscosity.

I laid your name out in brown Sea Belts and Sugar Kelpdecorated with paisley swirls of china fragments and small curved shells,
like new born baby's toes, sand dusted and salt encrusted.
Lunch was foraged Razor Clams fried in a skillet over an open fire,
with a knob of my Mother's hand churned butter.

I toasted you with Malbec from a tin mug, reflecting on temps passé.
At your home, the door ajar for the bantams to run in and out,
as if you had just gone to Chapel, or the post office.
The aroma of Lux flakes lingered around the twin tub,
and your Coal Tar soap still wet on the wooden draining board.
A pig's head soaking in a bucket of water with garlic and herbs,
brawn in the making, you didn't expect to leave us.
Beside the telephone, a bowl of bottle tops for guide dogs for the blind,
four knitting needles working their way around the heel of a sock,
a shrivelling apple core and a half-written letter to Wendy.

Wendy Falla

Flight

Here there is no room to stand or sit
so I'll kneel and sieve abandoned treasures:
the dolls we thought the start of a collection,
the notebooks full of wisdom of the dead,
my old school readers, fact and fancy
and further back, under brittle newspapers
headlining assassinations, landings, victories,
the statue I brought from home,
dusty, hands outstretched, refreshing.

When the media report me missing,
seek an angle to suit their new idolatries,
most neighbours will express shock,
say I was quiet, normal,
though some will claim to have always found me
a little odd, offbeat, too sensible.
The police will suspect I've broken down,
gone to ground in some high place, Ox Mountains
or somewhere between Ledbury and Worcester.
But I'll be here in my attic space,
the right hand side, nearest the setting sun,
rummaging through old stuff,
once leading-edge technology,

curled photographs and leaking soft toys,
enjoying the unfashionable, time-worn, reviving the
redundant, arranging lively tableaux before the still statue,
enjoying the serenity, silence, waiting.

Michael Farry

A Barrel of Monkeys

Grandad's Sideboard

The tipples beloved of many an aged aunt
Doilies and photographs, hibernating plants.
Hand crafted cutlery no one knows how to use
A button, a pin, a one hundred Amp fuse.

Tumblers, the colour of petrol adrift on a lake
Silver cake stands used only for Christenings and wakes.
Dishes made when manufacturing was art
and labourers were artists in sweet and hot glass.

A lifetime of random once precious luxurious things
a crib board with a match stick and an ornate silver pin
Keeping score from a game that no one alive can now win.
Board games and jigsaws, precious memories that sting.

Andy B J Low

87, 984.

He died alone near here
Or was it some other place?
Maybe the hearse passed
and you glanced briefly
not realising you knew his face.

He died alone. Near here,
people too often do.
There were four people at his funeral
did he once live next door to you?

He died alone near here
upon his coffin I scattered earth
and so did the three others attending.
That's one of us for every
nineteen years since his birth.

He died, alone.
Does it really matter where?
And that so many others
did not choose to care?

And, like them I have lived
thousands of my days through
being guilty of choosing
not to care too?

Gareth Toms

Space for Christina

Christina tumbles home, from guiding others'
children to watch the rim of a petal
with eyes closed, and contact
gently the heaving canvas. Offer her

the heron's hidden face undreaming
under feathers limbed in lunar silver,
reflected where its ripples disappeared.

Day's wading melts in the liquid West,
the city's popcorn chorus cleansed
in orange, gold, purple, black depth
washing into the ocean.

Eyes closed she touches the petal,
wet on paper, brushes the listening night
along the shore of sleep, awake
in cool dark she inks a note
to a lover she meets in dreams.
Offer her the deep of starlit streams.

Marcus Belassie

The spaces between

We probably need them...
The pauses between words

The ellipses in thoughts
The crass caesura in a world of
run on lines
The gap between a title and it's
extended metaphor
The empty parking spaces

The passageways and corridors
Like a synapse to the dendrite.

They're the centre of a whirlwind
The heavens before it rains
The lightning before the thunder or
An opened briefcase
It's the empty oven
The nobody's home
The space between
The matrix of a bone

A Barrel of Monkeys

The sigh
The yawn
The midday nap
The i before its dot
The blanks left on a
Crossword
The spill before its spot
The fingers moving between keys
The bullet before it's shot

For these are all but bridges
Like oceans and like seas
That join the ever solid -
Land of epiphanies
Yes

These are the spaces between matter or
What matters

Bianca Hendicott

The Butcher

'I killed a man, once,' he said
Pink and white fingers
Weigh out minced beef
Before swaddling it in white paper, bloodstained.
'A pound of sausages please.'
If he was joking it was poor taste
His smile was friendly still
Teeth uneven
'It was war.'
Pale sausages like a man's hand
Lump into white paper
'I had to tell someone.'

I pull my purse from my basket
'And six slices of bacon.'
'I had to use my bayonet
My gun jammed.'
Slices of greenback fall evenly
I count change
He is lying.
'Will that be all today?'
'Yes, thank you.' My fingers touch his
As I hand over notes and coins

He's lying
My eyes meet his still blue gaze
And I know
He is telling the truth.

Trisha Broomfield

The Elephant in the Living Room

The elephant in the living room
Well it was an orphan you see
It looked out at me with twinkling
Mischievous eyes, flapped its ears
And curled its trunk as though surprised
To have been born with such an appendage
On its smiley face
The next thing I knew
It had put one foot through the TV screen and planted it
Followed by three others
Onto my newly laid carpet
What followed was chaos
The elephant in the living room
Gleefully overturned the coffee table
Littering magazines like multi-coloured stepping-stones
Then it knocked over the standard lamp
The one we rescued from the skip
And twirled towards the dining table scattering bills and receipts Like confetti
Now don't get me wrong, it's cute, the elephant in the living room
And it has lost its mum
The mischievous eyes would melt the hardest heart
The smile would soften stone
But it is the other end with which we have issues
My carpet won't stand up to the treatment it has begun to receive
Anyway what do elephants eat?

And where is it going to sleep?
It is too large for the cat flap that's for sure
The trouble is it broke our TV screen on the way here
And I can't send it back.

Trisha Broomfield

At the Chemist's

The lady at the Chemist's is extremely small,
neater than ninepence, dressed in navy blue.
A crisp white blouse, or maybe an overall,
sticks out in an official manner under her cardigan,
her fringe, wisp free and ruler straight,
her glasses steady at the tip of her tiny nose.

In between looking after people in the shop,
"Yaas, just ten minutes, quarter of an hour"
she scans her world, and with minutest care
straightens a wayward bottle jostling on the shelf,
stands back a little, checking each label, faces forward as it should
till symmetry is exact, no gaps to fill.

There is a shelf too high for her to reach
somewhere out of sight must be a hidden stool
(Preparations for stools are ranged in perfect order on her shelves,
With plasters, linament, lotions, potions for face and neck,
linctus to shut the baby up at night,
and various creams for problems " lower down.")

Outside, across the road, some daffodils are doing their best.
All the surrounding grass is curbed In Its desire to wander
by discreet municipal edging- not too high,
lest idiot members of the public might trip over it, and fall,
subsequently suing the Council. (You never know,
there might be money in it.)

A Barrel of Monkeys

The flowers are dragooned to form a square,
so close together, they must stand upright,
discouraging boys on bicycles, resisting hurricanes,
doing their duty to beautify the Borough.
They make a perfect carpet,
or rather, mat, in unrelieved suburban yellow.

Inside, the little lady pops from behind her counter,
the colour of her stockings and her shoes
exactly matching skirt and cardigan (skirt just below the knee),
to re-arrange some bottles on a further shelf.
To my surprise, her weeny navy feet have flighty bows like
butterflies,
alighting an instant on some unlikely flower.

It seems quite possible that when she leaves the shop,
as clouds are pink and gold in the fading light,
she'll cross the road, and in the bosky woods
just visible behind the bungalows,
she'll kick up her tiny navy knees,
her cardigan fluttering in the February breeze,
and she'll go dancing with the daffodils.

Caro Reeves

Sandwich Boy:
The Boy Born Between Bread

Little James was born between bread,
Granary to be exact.
Out stuck his arms, his legs, his head,
He was a sandwich and that is a fact.

When James grew older he went to school,
But hated every day.
He feared and loathed the other kids,
For what they'd do and say.

They called him names, played mean tricks,
And then would jeer and boast.
They once tied him to a radiator,
To see if he'd turn into toast.

It was times like this that made James sad,
But he soon came to fear for his life.
For one day the kids brought some butter to school,
Along with a sizeable knife.

They surrounded James when no one was there,
And cut off some of his crust.
They ate it right there, in front of his face,
With a vicious and sadistic lust.

A Barrel of Monkeys

As they ate more and more,
James lashed out with a punch.
But nothing was going to stop these kids,
From making James into their lunch.

They chopped him up and scoffed him down
Along with lashings of butter.
But one by one they started to choke,
To wheeze and cough and splutter.

These kids weren't used to granary bread,
For they usually only ate white.
With James's seeds lodged in their throats,
Their futures no longer seemed bright.

Unable to breathe they fell to the floor,
And lay still from their heads to their feet.
Our poor little James was the very last thing,
These nasty kids ever did eat.

Alex Crumbie

Eve

I have no idea why you are asking me,
when you yourself said that I was only a scrap of bone, a bit of rib,
it must be obvious, even to you, that I could have no thoughts to call my own.

Why you have never asked for my opinion is perfectly clear-
You have all the opinions, I just think the things I think,
We are, I imagine, meant to spend the day wandering hand in hand,
Which is relaxing, if a little dull.

I find that Paradise is very well and good,
it's fortunate we don't live further North,
and, as for providing lunch,
Why did whoever made us make us omnivorous?

Providing interesting food with bits of leaf,
and only certain fruits,
not even a potato, or some other roots,
having no spade, this I do not find easy.

We have no Fire.

A very sensible snake I met one day
wreathing herself around a forbidden tree
put the idea into my head. (It couldn't have been me,
being only a rib,) to try the rosy, glowing, tempting fruit.

A Barrel of Monkeys

Personally, I wasn't that upset
When we were turned away by that fellow with his flaming sword,
(why does he need a flaming sword, I ask myself,
when we are unarmed, disarmed, and with nothing on?

Hardly a threat, I would have thought,
to one with blazing face and wings of steel,)
But then, I'm only a rib covered in human flesh,
A most miraculous skeleton.

Anyway, in some ways it was quite a relief
to see that Adam had to pick up a fork and dig a field,
Getting his precious fig-leaf grubby,
just for a change.

I think I look quite dainty in my cottony leaves,
the snake gives me a wink, and slips into the wall
which, for some reason,
Archangels have built around our orchard.

It makes no kind of sense to me at all,
but then it wouldn't, being only a rib.
I'm all for a bit of ribbing,
I can take a joke,

But I must say, it hurts when I am cracked,
cracking a joke is one thing, but BABIES !
Who thought that one up?
As usual, himself gets off scot free,
babies are women's work, he says to me.

The disobedient snake refuses to eat dust.
Adam can never hit her with his spade,
just now and then, a frog goes missing from the pond,
as, smiling to herself,
she vanishes silently among the stones.

Caro Reeves

Volunteers 1

Groom of the Stool

Fuck it! Who used the last of the King's volunteers?

Came the cry from the cupboard under the stairs

The King stranded, trousers down, coat tails round his ears.

His arse needed wiping and nobody cared.

We were rolling in laughter and blinded with tears.

Getting used to exile. It's going to take a few years.

Andy B J Low

Volunteers 2.

From the audience please.

The animals were all eaten

The custard pies were all gone

The chair legs consumed by the lions, every one

And audience participation no longer an option

So the self-loading cannons fell silent, one by one.

Said the clown to the colonel, his face dripping with tears

"Sir. We're all out of volunteers."

And the war of the Circuses entered its final few years.

Andy B J Low

Bird Song Rhyme

Poetry is parrots.
Sentences are swans.
Words are wading water birds
Atop a moving pond.
All are flying colours
Inking through the sky
Where nests are made
And eggs are laid
And ideas never die.

Bianca Hendicott

Guest Poets

The second half of the Barrel of Monkeys is devoted to poems by a few of the writers who have read as featured poets at our events in Guildford, or who have written poems that we particularly like, including our competition judge, Alwyn Marriage. We hope you enjoy them too. I've also taken the opportunity to include three poems of my own and three by Dónall Dempsey, my partner in all the 1000 Monkeys projects and host of our performance events and readings.

Janice Windle

A Barrel of Monkeys

Six impossible things before breakfast

Like what?
demanded Alice.
Well … the white queen hesitated
trying to formulate something
that was obviously impossible
but that she could imagine, (ignorant
of the fact that a number of philosophers
have grappled with this problem
over the years).

Then, grasping each finger in turn
as she enumerated, she began:

1. I expect you think that when the sun
goes down, no one can read a book,
because the light from oil lamps and from
candles is too dim. But I manage to believe
that everyone could flick a little switch
that would instantly illuminate
all the rooms within their house,
making night as bright as day.

2. With a little more effort
it's possible to believe
that you and I could be
transported at enormous speed
to Timbuktu and back
without the aid of horse
and carriage.

3. It's possible, you know,
to keep a tiny pet machine
on which to imprint messages
that can be simultaneously read
on the far side of the world
(if anyone there happens to be sitting
at their desk, rather than slumbering
in bed).

4. If I try hard enough
I can even believe it's possible
to send a strange-shaped vehicle
into outer space
and land it accurately on a comet
over two hundred and sixty
million miles away.

5. I stubbornly believe
that countries that go to war,

slay millions of each other's citizens,
lay waste to the most beautiful cities,
breed distrust and engender hate,
can, within a few short years,
learn to respect each other and join
in a peaceful union of nations.

6. And this morning I even believed
that a little girl could pass through glass
into my realm, and then expect
to get away without losing her head.

Alice gave the queen a quizzical look,
and as she plotted her escape
(hoping, rather than believing,
that it was possible), decided
that if she ever made it back
to normal life, instead of daydreaming
she'd study science and engineering.

Alwyn Marriage

First published in *The Alice in Wonderland Anthology,*

Silver Birch Press, California, 2015.

Visiting Speaker

An Australian friend
who came to Britain
to speak at a clergy conference

felt lonely, isolated, odd,
and believing it was best to give feed-back
electrified the assembled company

with an Aussie expression;
told them she felt like
a shag on the rocks.

Alwyn Marriage
First published in *The Broadsheet*, autumn 2015

Reading the signs

Travelling westwards on the M4 motorway
a sign instructs us to '*Turn R for the Oracle*'.
Will there, I wonder, be queues to consult
this Delphic sage? and can I ask
what my future holds?

Along the lane there's evidence of recent
road works, and another sign that reads
***Cats' Eyes Removed.* I wonder what**
a foreigner's supposed to make of that;
is it a threat or promise?

Alwyn Marriage

First published in *Notes from a Camper Van*

Me in my Ho Chi Minh sandals

You can kill ten of my men for every one I kill of yours,
but even at those odds you will lose and I will win.
Ho Chi Minh, 1945

I shed inches, become compact,
agile; my body supple as elastic
so I can fold-up flat
like that contortionist beggar.

The muscles in my calves
are knotted rope. I can squat
on my haunches for hours,
turn the unexploded shells

of my enemy into lethal snares
to blast him. I sharpen bamboo
to the thickness of my wrists
which I will plant in the earth

to impale him when he false-
steps, as he will, on the shutters
of the window trap,
where he'll fall, to be spiked
for his foolishness. My eyes
are ovals of onyx set

in porcelain pleats of skin.
They pierce the dark

as I wolf-lope through the caves,
bent double, join my comrades
in the planning room, drink tea
from bone-thin china—sharpen

our senses—drink to peace
as if we do not know how long
it will take, how many of us
will die waiting. But we are many,

slip into each other's rubber sandals
with silent ease. In the cause
of freedom, we bond
under the mantel

of our collective imagination.
Victory cannot be far away.
In my Ho Chi Minh sandals
I know I can walk that far.

Wendy Klein

First published in *Ware Poetry Competition anthology* after winning 1st prize in 2009

Going without Saying

Tie your scarf under your chin, brisk and taut; hang your
apron
on the hook above the stove, its mouth wide open and
empty,

stained black with family fires, the handles of the pots
torqued
into unlikely shapes. The stepping stones don't know

you've swept your last; that the moss has already sown its
seeds. Just
walk away from the sad-eyed shutters, painted pink when
you thought

you might stay on. Walk past the Sweet Williams; they'll
only fade;
the Irises that shake their gaudy beards; leaf spikesfierce
as swords

grouped at their feet. Don't look back at that window pane,
splintered
when the first bombs fell, slivers raining down like crystal

on Baka's linen cloth, the silver hand-polished by Yelena,
bought cheap
in that Belgrade shop; the symmetry of your evening shattered.

Leave the door open; there's nothing left to steal – just
paint peeling
in brown flakes like dried blood. Turn your back on the arch

with its faded paper bows, mementos of your wedding day.
Walk fast
past the photos of your recent dead, draped with floral
tributes in plastic

to last forever. Slip between the stone lions, their gaze that
gives
away nothing. Walk right away from the rub of sack cloth,

the sprinkle of ashes, creamy saucers of elderflower, edible
mimosa.
Leave the wind to spread the news.

Wendy Klein
First published in Wendy's collection, *Cuba in the Blood* .

Havana

She's an old whore, who drags
her soiled petticoats,
through the moist dark.

The leather seats of her taxis are cracked
by old trysts, the fenders dented
by bodies from another time.

She side-steps around young girls
in stilettos, out late looking for work
finding it, their tawny legs

insinuated between
the thighs of men who were
weary just minutes ago,

but no longer, as their flies are
fingered, their grizzled pates stroked by
warm hands, their backs pressed tight

against rusty wrought-iron gates,
leaving a filigree imprint that
will remind them tomorrow

of rumba in Havana.
The red light of her cigarillo moves,
and with each inhalation,

flashes a tight Morse code: the sting
of the smoke, the flare of her nostrils,
more sensed than seen. She's a lady dragon

and she'll take them inside her hot tunnel mouth,
sear their flesh with her cinnamon tongue,
musky and wise with nicotine;

brown with the last smoke of evening,
before lying down, and the first smoke of morning,
before lying down again.

Smoke, she hums, gets in your eyes, and
sly as the rising breeze brushing bare flesh,
the palm leaves will croon the chorus.

Wendy Klein
First published in Wendy's collection, *Cuba in the Blood*

This Room In The Sunlight

This room in the sunlight
and music weaving,
imploring from the other room.
And Erica! Her silhouette perched
over the newspaper,
sighing for the woes of the world.
Then she turns, her sadness, her smiles
coalesce, dance together
in those deep dark eyes.
This room in the morning.
And birds, the other side of glass
darting through bare branches.
And the music slowly, slowing,
sewing sweet threnody.
This room in the sunlight.
Work soon. Not now.
Soon, after coffee.
And my fingertips restless,
waiting.
But the web of sunlight
enclosing, disabling the turmoil,
the turbine of my brain.
This room in the morning,

and my heart full of loving.
And the calling laughter
of children not here.
And the lingering, echoing;
and Erica there
haloed by Sunlight,
pouring gold into this space called
Home.
Into this room in the sunlight
and the joy of living.

Bernard Kops

Peace

Our kids have just left home.
We gave them all our love,
they raided all our dreams
and ate up all our jam,
and left us just like that;
laughed all down the road.
Our kids have just left home.
And oh the sweet relief,
come, let's postpone our grief
and please answer the phone.
They're coming three o'clock?
And staying for the night?
Where did we go right?

Bernard Kops

The Myrtle Bush

The myrtle bush
Sings in the garden
Under a black night
When I open the door
she embraces me.
I close my eyes
And pull two leaves
from her branches
and rub them between my fingers.
The perfume of the far off
desert garden
assails the cold night air.
Flute and tambour dance me
into the communal garden.
Anyone peeping from the high
moon windows
must think I'm mad.
As I turn, faster and faster,
round and round
Over the wet grass.

Bernard Kops

At the Casa de Rebolfe

Singly.

Spiralling down a plumb-line of gravity
a polished leaf

descends from the orange tree.

We talk. Read books.

Beyond
the tamed and passive Douro dreams
reflecting on her reedy glass
all she consumed; a drowned geography
of farms once hoed,
homesteads and terraced vineyards,
olive groves, that drop to where
her turbulent original
spumed over granite in the valley cleft.

We talk. Read books.

Cherish the shade.

A dragonfly settles,
measures a turquoise inch of time
between grass-blade and grass-blade

as if in time, he could measure all of it,
afternoon by sultry afternoon
under the planetary oranges.

Chrys Salt

Douro – A river flowing W from N central Spain, it forms part of the border between Spain and Portugal before entering the Atlantic Ocean at Oporto.

First published in The Galloway Poets Series Vol 4 Markings 1996

The gap between my fingers

The gap between my fingers

stops me in my tracks
I wear my father's hands
big knuckles dating time
like tree rings

grief does not mend
it grows a scab on pain
a smelly cheese, buffed shoes ,
a cactus in a pot
linseed
a stranger's ears or nose
will knock it off
to bare the wound
again

they say hands are the giveaway

and I remember his
holding a pen
a book
a Players No.10
or folded in his lap
on the day of the diagnosis
knowing the train had left the station

that it was the last one home.

Chrys Salt
First published in *Greedy for Mulberries (*Markings 2008*)*

Lost (Iraq: March 2003)

**There are no maps for poets in this country.
The compass finger, mindless on its post
will not direct us on this dangerous journey.
An unfamiliar landscape tells us we are lost.
Above the bramble and the rambling wood
the wheeling dragons search for bones
of luckless travellers who have misconstrued
the alien symbols on the milestones.
We have nowhere to go but where we are, our options
closed, the exit double locked.
We may not take direction from a star.
The stars are out and all the roads are blocked.
How can we dare this nightmare territory,
the shifting contours of the hills and coasts,
the gibberish signposts and the season's enmity.
What hand our touchstone in this land of ghosts?**

Chrys Salt MBE

First published in *Grass (IDP 2012)*

The Trouble With a Parent Dying When You Are a Child

is that you don't say goodbye, don't know what goodbye
means. Even the hellos haven't been said properly.

Here are fragments: a bedside story, a present,
a smile – tinged yellow and faded. Is that who
you're saying goodbye to?

Where is the celebration? Everyone is asleep
afraid of the morning.
The new day creeps in uninvited. Tears are
in a cupboard waiting to be worn.

In the background, someone is laughing
at an old family joke that used to be funny

and everyone is too frightened to explain,
as if death stole the punchline.

Eventually you take just one day and pretend
it doesn't hurt – allow yourself to sing, to chuckle.

He was a very funny man.

Hannah Linden

The Body

For my brother, 'Adil

The wisdom of silence
is over.
Those terrible times
are over.
The importance of the body
is over
the agony of the mass graves

begins.

Let me say something about you.
We know this.
You were born in Baghdad in 1964
You were arrested on Friday
April 11th 1980

We do not know if or how you died.
Since earth does not deserve you
heaven takes that responsibility.
Your stainless soul
Is fit for nothing less
You have risen like a phoenix from the ash.

'Ghareeb Iskander

(Translated from the Arabic by Chrys Salt and the author.)

Of You

When I think of you,
who even in those terrible, dark times
showed no emotion,
shed not one single tear..
Now you tell me
the hardships of exile are too hard to bear.

Let me tell you this!
There is only one real exile.
That is exile from life itself.

Don't kid yourself.
Life is an illusion,
We are all narratives
wandering through camps of self-deception.
Prisons of endurance,
Tombs for a last breath.

So I reclaim my memories.
Reject your refusal to remember.

How could you say nothing about all that destruction
Yet weep now at the damage done to a small rose?

In the garden we share
the three of us
there is just you.
me
and The Cross.

'Ghareeb Iskander

England

Straight off the bat let me say
I was never a fan
I mean don't speak ill and all that
but if we're clearing the decks
wiping the slate clean
getting it all out in the open
then....
you were bloody hard work, England,
not easy to live with, let alone love.

You see, you kept making me and my friends
sit cricket tests I was never going to pass
took our taxes and our labour
but still left us feeling second class
because our roots stretched back
to other cultures, other shores
and other teams made our guilty, secret hearts
beat a little faster, race a little more.
Even now, it's like you can't help yourself
some scoundrel starts waving the flag
critical thought goes out of the window
and next thing you know
you've tanked yourself up on bigotry and lager
giving it *'2 world wars and 1 world cup'*
like you fired the winning shot yourself.
I mean really, England? Really?
I've seen you running for the bus

**in the mornings, and it's not pretty.
You're a heart attack waiting to happen
hypertension, clogged arteries, dodgy knees
it's all history, for fuck's sake
do yourself a favour, let it go.**

**And you were the chink of fine china
the tyranny of manners and the old school tie
tut-tut-tutting about the enemy within
turning a blind eye while someone
did your dirty work
gratuitous truncheons
battles in beanfields
cover-ups and never-challenged lies.
So, like I say, it wasn't the best of starts.
I had to leave to learn to love you
get far enough away to see both sides
of the coins in your pocketful of shrapnel
find the fist that read *'love'*
not just the one that promised *'hate'*.**

**And out there,
on the other side of the world
I found I missed you
missed your dirt under my fingernails
hankered after your way with words
your dirty laugh
your seaside postcard humour
and your beautiful mongrel language.
Every time you open your mouth
history tumbles from your lips**

in dialect and accent
a pulsing archaeology of trade
invasion, conquest, immigration
the ebb and flow of populations
making room making homes
and getting assimilated
learning there's precious few of life's problems
not cut down to size with another cup of tea
and a couple of biccies.

You're not dead.
You're just evolving
re-inventing yourself
getting your nails done
putting on your glad rags
for a night out on the town
and I will find you
on top of the moors
quoting Benny Hill and Shakespeare
feasting on samosas and flagons of cider
slapping the taut drum of your stomach
where it spills over the waistband of your trousers
– *all paid for, kid!* –
proud as punch
Falstaff, as I live and breathe
paddling in the shallows
beyond the deckchairs and the donkeys
giggling in Gujerati
the hem of your sari trailing in the cold North Sea
salty and wet while your wide-eyed kids
play shoot-em-up in the arcades

mither you for fish and chips
support City and United
and ride the bus home
with their heads full of dreams

knowing love triumphs
over cricket tests
and their hearts beat
proud and strong.

Steve Pottinger

The stunt

The director wanted me to do it which I wasn't happy about,
I prefer to supervise these days.
The scene called for me to jump from an open window;
they only had boxes to land on, I wanted foam.
We were behind schedule so I said fine,
but this pissed me off, it was unprofessional.
And I thought know what, I'll give 'em a little scare,
I won't get up straight away, afterward I'll lay still.
The actor had his close up, I step in, the camera behind me,
the director called action I made the jump.

Then wait still, open one eye,
but it's not my point of view, it's an overhead shot.
I see an assistant shake me by the shoulder
then look at the director; others rush over.
I see this as from a crane shot now, it pulls further back.

Bryan Baker

One Kind of Worm

Solitary children often grow strange,
crouching in hedges, skulking through streams.
They might mature, but they never change;
the wild will always hold appeal, the range
will always call them away from work or teams.
Solitary children often grow strange —
they have adventures with mental ghosts. Pages
fly beneath their fingers, fueling fire-dreams.
They mature, but they never change.
Escapism is easy. Find a tree. Forrage
through the branches, peeling bark until something gleams.
Solitary children often grow strange,
they find unexpected doors that lead away from rage, light
roads leading out of the world — bright streams.
These children mature, but they never change;
long-legged, dark-eyed, they stalk the stage
or learn to type. They know the world is not what it seems.
Solitary children often grow strange;
they might mature but they never change.

Bethany Pope

Mother Fingers the Edge of the Sea

It was not feeling that was the problem
or even not feeling. It was having something
to feel about.... again! Soft like sand, her fingers
loosening. Grass days, housemartins under the eaves,
there's a pattern formed early. *I will not, I will not...*

She: like a radio, always tuned to the same station.
Under my skin, years water the child and she grows.
Love sits, silvering like a glue-gun. This dress is a map.
It knows which hills to climb. My brother told me
I am too different for him to know. Dark words

collar the sofa. Smoke-music yellows the ceiling.
Your stone heart seemed ready but mine was not.

Hannah Linden

Just a Pigeon

the trees hide the orchestra
behind green and brown
the sun gazes past the clouds
like film behind cautious shutters

the town dulls and brightens
in this intermittent light display
as the avian band sets
the mood

the audience in this theatre
talk quietly throughout the show
they take pictures to prove
that their eyes can still see

a child, leaning and bouncing
off the wooden barrier, announces
'look mum, mum look!
a bird is in that tree,
can you see?'

the mum looks over the
camera's viewfinder
and looks where her child sees

'oh, darling' the mum asserts
'that's just a pigeon'

'oh' the child replies,
looking at the branches
framing the sky
where a wonder used to be.

Alex Twyman

Like Music Made Visible

You forever always

like music
made visible

running through my thoughts
memory's shaky home movie

here a grinning granny
with half a head most of the time

or an uncle
with a cloud upon his head

there the camera elects
to look at only the grass

or an aunt always on the edge
of a frame

quiet but not quite
one of the almost theres

an uncle represented by
his shiny new shoes

and a sudden falling
shot of skies

and a passing bird
these black and white people

in their black and white world

moving through silence
as if they were swimming

through time
flirting now

or shying from
the camera's gaze

as the footage comes
to an abrupt:

stop.

But you forever always
like music

made visible.

Dónall Dempsey

She Forgets to Brush her Teeth Yet Again

Rain was falling
as she was falling

asleep.

Strangely the cuckoo clock
didn't cuckoo

as it would
usually do.

The canary who
usually too

broke into a terrible
chatter

at being usurped
by an absurd bird of wood

terrible chattered
not.

She felt as if
a million of her

were falling falling

and the rain

had finally fallen

asleep.

Sunshine tapped
her on the shoulder

and a new morning
offered itself to her

with such a graciousness that
goodness gracious she

could not possibly
refuse.

Somewhere in her
head the rain

still lay asleep.

She did her best
not to

wake it

Dónall Dempsey

How the Black Shines

He remembers
the particular
glance of sunlight
off a bird's wing

so that the black
shone
for that second
and forever

and how he had stolen it
from the living tapestry

of that only moment
and if one were to go back

it would be found
to be missing

thieved from Time
and how now

the typewriter keys
raise their angry little fists

and strike the page
in rage

and the tiny ting when a word comes
to the end of a line

and the stolen sunshine and
the shining of black

become
the words

that are offered
now

this seeing at seven
become a bird of words

startled to find itself now
on the snowdrift
of a page

snatched from the memory
of a child who is

no longer a child

Dónall Dempsey

It was Dark When they Met

Their lips were small crabs
searching a shell
Salt was their sweetness
and dry
their seahorse tongues.

Her breath was made of candle glow.
He could not extinguish her
so
he waited for her
to blow over.

His tongue was a tsunami
she was the shore laid waste.

That night

pearl divers
were the only survivors.

Janice Windle

It Was Dark When They Parted

bells tolled
told him her promise
was paper and wax
not currency not
iron-clad not
a licence to kill
nor a reason to live.

He left her with
a cool hand
and the stacked cards
rose up in a pack
clattered
like knucklebones at his feet.

The sun climbed its shattered stair
there was no more chiming
her promises were
wax and paper
he was held

sealed
ignited
and razed
to the charred earth.

Janice Windle

Politics for Animals

How to be a sheep:
Grow a thick fleece. Be thankful when you're shorn of it,
Obey anyone with a whistle and a dog,
Keep your head down
and your mouth full.

How to be a goat:
Toss your knucklebone head in protest
when you're tethered,
Kick up your clicketty feet and dance when you're free,
Digest everything that's thrown at you.

How to be a shoat:
Grow your hair long but never get fleeced.
Throw up your hands and what can't be digested.
Keep your feet on the ground.
Love goats. Love sheep.

Janice Windle

Key to the photos on the back cover

ABOUT THE POETS

Bryan Baker lives and works in South London, and often reads at open mics. His main hobby is lounging about, which takes up most of his free time; and much of the rest.

Marcus Belassie has worked as a writer since 2011, primarily in theatre as resident poet/playwright/grammar monkey for Alma Studios in Surrey. He has now stumbled sideways into performance poetry, and consults on literary theory for Alma's external LAMDA exams. He has two cats, called Baggins and Mephistopheles.

Trisha Broomfield: "when I was younger I was told off for day-dreamimg, now people just ask what planet I'm on. I have always had a sense of the ridiculous. Sometimes it shows in my pottery, sometimes it comes out in my drawing but mostly it wriggles out in my writing."

Alicia Buller is full time editor of the sustainable business magazine Salt. She's also a part time writer of poetry and contemporary short stories based on our modern world and relationships. She lived in Dubai for seven years before returning to the UK in 2014.

Jim Carter performs under the name of the Tramping Artisan. Born in Oldham, when younger he was involved in the Manchester music scene. He has been fortunate to have worked in a number of areas: a tram driver, a prison custody officer, a psychotherapist and is a One Spirit Interfaith Minister and Spiritual Counsellor. Now living in Godalming Surrey, he works as a business consultant in a variety of people related areas.

Joy Parry Collins occasionally writes poetry whilst looking after a home of overgrown children. She started in Advertising, after a degree in English Lit, got side-tracked by a marriage and continued her (life) education in Tunisia, Nigeria, Scotland and the US. She returned to Surrey where she is in the final stages of writing her first novel. She enjoys singing, piano, acting, walking, talking and Dostoyevsky.

Alex Crumbie's poems usually tell short, humorous stories, which are aimed at adults, children and everyone in between. After writing a number of these tales, he realised that many of them end with the main character dying. At first this realisation caused him some concern, but he later decided that death is actually the most natural conclusion.

Dónall Dempsey has been the host of The 1000 Monkeys' spoken word events in Guildford, Surrey, since 2011. He is the author of three collections and his poems have been published widely in print and online journals and anthologies. Some have been translated into Spanish, Italian and Hindi. He has taken part in festivals in Ireland, France and India.

Ray Diamond long ago conceived the ingenious plan of becoming famous by eschewing publicity. It has yet to bear fruit. He has been published extensively in *The Delinquent* (now defunct), as well as *South Bank Poetry, Ariadne's Thread* and *Fuselit.* He is the author of a full collection of verse published by Black Box, which has sold very many copies and been generally well received.

Susan Evans is a Brighton-based performance poet from north-east London. Straddling stage and page, Susan's widely published in independent magazines and journals; in print and online. `I write to taste life twice' said Anais Nin, Susan penned Barcelona in that same vein; inspired by a trip in 2015. *Barcelona* first appeared in the inaugural edition of the *High Window* online journal.

Wendy Falla writes poetry, flash, long and short fiction, lyrics, music and a blog. Influenced by her Channel Island up-bringing, her writing is nostalgic, often melancholic: scenes of times past, which at times appear other worldly. Wendy lives on a farm with 7 rescue dogs and a parrot.

Michael Farry is Irish and writes poetry and history. His first poetry collection, *Asking for Directions*, was published by Doghouse Books in 2012. His history book, *Sligo, The Irish Revolution 1912-1923*, was published in 2012 by Four Courts Press. He is fascinated by the amount of poetry published in some local Irish newspapers in the 1912-1923 period.

Andy V Frost: "Biker and Poet from outer S.W. London. Getting a bit frayed around the edges for his age now but is still prone to wanderlust and fond of visiting Poetry events unannounced." On his poem "the Northern Line" : "A personal view of the London Underground line from a lifelong Morden (its Southern terminus) resident."

Ivor Hartney is a performance poet with a beautiful voice. He loves the theatre.

Bianca Hendicott: A review described her early poems as: "A dish for Hannibal Lecter prepared by Nigella Lawson, perhaps?" After a move from media to law to teaching and motherhood, we can safely say her more recent poems contain the same element of intrigue but with a more satisfying sustenance; all of which is spiced occasionally by her upbringing in South Africa. Delectable...

'Ghareeb Iskander was born in Baghdad. He studied Arabic literature at the University of Baghdad and poetry translation at the University of London. He published eight books including *A Chariot of Illusion* (London 2009); *Gilgamesh's Snake* (Beirut 2012); *Translating Sayyab into English* (London 2013). He has taken part in Erbil, Reel, Edinburgh, Wigtown, Bath and Niniti festivals, and Movement Against Xenphobia Conference. Ghareeb was the featured writer of Scottish Pen 2014.

Karen Izod, academic and writer, works as a consultant to organisations facing social and cultural change. Her poetry has been published in Agenda, Attachment, New Welsh Review's video showcase, and karnacology.com. In 2015 Karen was invited to participate in the Spirit of Place exhibition, St Mary's Church Morden, and wrote a sequence of 9 poems 'Mary', celebrating the 900th anniversary of the founding of the church. She is a lover of birds and wild places.

Wendy Klein, U.S.-born retired Psychotherapist, has lived in the U.K. most of her adult life. Despite dashing about between four daughters and twelve grandchildren, she has published *Cuba in the Blood*)2009), *Anything in Turquoise* (2013), and *Mood Indigo* (2016). She workshops with peer poets in Oxford, Swindon and Reading.

Bernard Kops, born in 1926, is one of the great post-war Jewish writers. He is a poet, novelist and one of the best-known playwrights of his generation. He has written more than forty plays for stage and radio, many of which have been broadcast worldwide, nine novels and seven volumes of poetry. he is also the author of an acclaimed autobiography.

Hannah Linden was part of Jo Bell's 52 group and subsequently has been published in several journals including Prole; Domestic Cherry; and Ink, Sweat and Tears. She was commended in the 2014 Prole Laureate. She and Gram Joel Davies won the Cheltenham Poetry Festival Compound Poem Competition 2015.

Andy B J Low says:
Who am I? No one knows. Professional idiot I suppose.
Romantic tart, tender heart. I love beautiful things.
That'll do for a start.
But be careful what else you ask of me.
The clue's in the e-mail: Dr.Evil.Phd(@outlook.com

Jeremy Loynes: “I have enjoyed writing since school days thanks to several inspirational teachers. In poetry, I like the challenge of trying to capture the essence of a thought or idea in a few lines. I write about whatever’s on my mind but one common theme is the natural world and our relationship with it. Influences include Edward Thomas and Robert Frost.”

Alwyn Marriage has been a university lecturer, chief executive of two NGOs, Editor of a journal and an Environmental Consultant. Three of her seven published books have been poetry, and her work appears frequently in magazines and anthologies. She is now Managing Editor of Oversteps Books, holds a research fellowship at the University of Surrey, was Poet in Residence for the Winchester 10 Days Arts Festival 2013 and gives readings all over Britain and abroad. www.marriages.me.uk/alwyn.htm

Kyle McHale is a geography and history teacher who has taught in the United States, and now lives and teaches locally in Guildford. Kyle has always had an interest in reading and writing poetry, believing that spoken word is a much-needed form of expression.

Owen Osler: "For years I have read and enjoyed poetry. Sometimes I would try to commit something to verse but the results were so embarrassing I threw them away. Only since last May 2015, with the help of my wife and my good friend Martin Jones, have my attempts at poetry escaped the waste paper basket."

Rochelle Parker devotes her life to pairing the socks, cooking proper dinners, and trapping locust-swarms of domestic paperwork in box-files. In the interstices afforded by intervals in the long-running Drama of Family, she writes poetry.

Geoffrey Pimlott is a painter and a member of the British Watercolour Society. Still a successful water-colourist, he says, "As my poetry has developed over the last eight years my work has reflected on events in the world, either as protest or as ironic observation, more and more, and the written word has become the means of communicating these thoughts and ideas."

Lorri Pimlott lives in the Surrey Hills. She was partly brought up in New Zealand and Australia, and has since lived in Papua New Guinea, Thailand and France. She often draws on her experiences of these widely-different cultures in her poetry. Other sources of inspiration include her interest in history and her love of plants.

Ray Pool: "My flirtation with poetry blossomed whilst working at the BBC. I had a poem published in Breakthru Magazine run by Ken Geering. It is only since semi – retiring from the music business that I have ventured into live poetry reading. Now a prolific writer, I tend to choose subject matter with a quirky or satirical aspect, often read with accents."

Bethany W Pope is an award-winning writer. She received her MA in Creative Writing from Trinity, Carmarthen, and her PhD from Aberystwyth University. She has published four poetry collections; A Radiance (Cultured Llama, 2012), Crown of Thorns (Oneiros Books, 2013), The Gospel of Flies (Writing Knights Press, 2014), and Undisturbed Circles (Lapwing, 2014). Her first novel, Masque, has been accepted by Seren Press and will be released in June of 2016.

Steve Pottinger is one of the most powerful and sincere voices in the political poetry arena, but is also capable of delivering moments of lyrical beauty...Based in the West Mids, he performs in clubs and pubs and at festivals, and is chief exec of grassroots poetry organisation Write Out Loud. You can read more of his work – and information about his gigs – at stevepottinger.co.uk

Caroline Reeves is Anglo-Irish, brought up in the Republic. Reluctantly, her parents allowed her to go to Chelsea School of Art, provided she learned to be a secretary first, just in case. She represented Ireland at the Deuxieme Biennale in Paris in 1961. She has written all her life, but privately. She sang a lot. She enjoys gardening, eavesdropping, and being asleep. Her poems have been published in *South* and *Artemis* literary journals.

Chrys Salt MBE is an award-winning poet, playwright and performer. Her work has been performed and broadcast widely. She was awarded an MBE for services to The Arts in Dumfries and Galloway in The Queen's Birthday Honours List 2014. She is the Artistic Director of the Bakehouse, a flourishing arts venue in South West Scotland. Her seventh collection, *"Dancing on a Rock"*, was published in 2015.

Richard Sellwood became enchanted by the poems of W. B. Yeats at primary school and has loved poetry ever since. His own poems are often inspired by nature and the past; he enjoys experimenting with language and form. Richard has just completed a fantasy novel, 'The Time Talker'. He co-founded The Cranleigh Writers' Group in 2006 and lives in Ewhurst.

Pauline Sewards co-hosts a poetry night in Bristol called Satellite of Love. She has been widely published in small press magazines including *South Bank Poetry* and online at *Ink, Sweat & Tears, Blue of Noon* and *I am not a silent poet*. More about Pauline is at http://www.writeoutloud.net/profiles/paulinesewards

Colonel Shyam Sunder Sharma, Shaurya Chakra (Retired), a decorated and war-wounded veteran, single parent to two daughters and two dogs, Shyam is an avid birdwatcher and nature lover. He holds a Master's degree in English Literature. Published in a number of anthologies and magazines in India and abroad, he goes by the alias Driftwood Ashore on Facebook, where he also runs a vibrant group - Poets, Artists Unplugged.

Gareth Toms: "I have been seriously writing poetry for over half my life. Trying to capture my thoughts, views, and my experiences, or creating characters who narrate their own journeys and communicate their experiences. My poem in this anthology is titled *'87, 984'* which is the plot number in a sprawling cemetery where a family friend is buried. He had an interesting life, but who else would know that?" Gareth is Vice-Chairman of Tongues & Grooves poetry club in Portsmouth.

Alex Twyman is believed to be one of the 'Special 12' that the 12 true Gods bestowed upon the world as dawn shattered the sleeping on the 2nd of October 1985. Alex is the offspring of the Aztec god Huehuecoyotl, and must rescue the humans from their false idols and ideologies with drink, music, poetry, stories, and dance.

Kathy Tytler is a slow long distance runner from Reading who often draws inspiration for her poetry from the landscape she runs through, or from the simple experience of running. She is 'poet in residence' at Ed & Phil's running events; 'The Poets' Paths Marathon' and 'Running Order' in Dymock. She also enjoys reading her poems about Reading.

Sarah Watkinson, @philonotis, is a lifelong scientist and recent poet. Her work (mostly done as a student of The Poet's House, Oxford, and as a member of Jo Bell's 52 group) is in *Antiphon, Ink Sweat* and *Tears,*

Pennine platform, *The Rialto* and *Well Versed* and has won several prizes. She lives in Oxfordshire.

John Wheeler has been a familiar face on the London spoken word scene for many years and has performed features for Apples and Snakes, Boxed In, and many others. He describes himself as a standup poet. He likes things to be accessible so he never does poems about the nature of art, camels, alienation, or meditations on the colour blue. (Though on second thoughts, he might reconsider camels...)

Janice Windle is a painter and local theatre reviewer who has had poems published in print and online anthologies and magazines. She enjoys making things happen, whether it's paintings, spoken word events or anthologies and collections like this one. She blogs on her three websites, www.dempseyandwindle.co.uk, www.janwindle.com and www.the1000monkeys.com.

www.ingramcontent.com/pod-product-compliance
Ingram Content Group UK Ltd.
Pitfield, Milton Keynes, MK11 3LW, UK
UKHW041937190726
13854UKWH00004B/1637

9 781907 435287